Gertrude Hall Brownell

Age of Fairygold

Gertrude Hall Brownell

Age of Fairygold

ISBN/EAN: 9783743309906

Manufactured in Europe, USA, Canada, Australia, Japa

Cover: Foto ©ninafisch / pixelio.de

Manufactured and distributed by brebook publishing software
(www.brebook.com)

Gertrude Hall Brownell

Age of Fairygold

BY

GERTRUDE HALL

AUTHOR OF "FAR FROM TO-DAY," "ALLEGRETTO," "FOAM
OF THE SEA," AND "THE HUNDRED
AND OTHER STORIES."

BOSTON

LITTLE, BROWN, AND COMPANY

1899

𝔘niversity 𝔓ress
John Wilson and Son, Cambridge, U. S. A.

TO MY MOTHER

CONTENTS

CONTENTS

CONTENTS

CONTENTS

CONTENTS

xi

Age of Fairygold

I

A FAIR King's-daughter once possessed
   A bird in whom she took delight;
And everything a bird loves best
   She gave this cherished one, but flight!

It was her joy to smoothe his wings,
   To watch those eyes that wax'd and wan'd,
To tender him choice offerings
   And have him feed from her white hand.

And every day she loved him more . . .
   But when at last she loved him most,
She opened wide his prison door,
   Content that he to her were lost.

I   I

II

THE night is black; the rain falls, fine,
  Incessant, vertical.
I stretch my arm through the dripping vine:
  I like to feel it fall.

I think of a garden that I know,
  Lying under this quiet rain:
The quince-tree blossoms vainly glow,
  The tulip's red in vain.

One color, petals now with stem,
  One bistre, green and pink:
Dear darkened flowers! I'm glad for them,
  They thirsted, they can drink.

III

I TRY to fix my eyes upon my book,
  But just outside a budding spray
Flaunts its new leaves as if to say,
    " Look! — look ! "

I trim my pen, I make it fine and neat;
  There comes a flutter of brown wings,
A little bird alights and sings,
    " Sweet! — sweet! "

O little bird, O go away! be dumb!
  For I must ponder certain lines ;
And straight a nodding flower makes signs,
    " Come! — come! "

O Spring, let me alone! O bird, bloom, beam,
  " I have no time to dream! " I cry;
The echo breathes a soft, long sigh,
    " Dream! — dream! "

3

IV

How shall we tell an angel
　From another guest?
How, from the common worldly herd,
　One of the blest?

Hint of suppressed halo,
　Rustle of hidden wings,
Wafture of heavenly frankincense, —
　Which of these things?

The old Sphinx smiles so subtly:
　" I give no golden rule, —
Yet would I warn thee, World : treat well
　Whom thou call'st fool."

V

The vine is barely in flower,
  And it's only the time for seed —
  But I claim, I ache for, I need,
My harvest this very hour.

O Mother, leave saying that thing!
  Does it make life better to bear
  To know that when Autumn is there
One is sure to weep for the Spring?

VI

When May paints azure all above,
And emerald all underfoot,
And charms to flower the withered root,
   And warms to passion the staid dove,
   Sing, bard! of hope, of joy, of love!

But when December saddens o'er
The land whence birds and leaves are gone,
When black nights come, and grey days dawn,
   Sing, bard! sing louder than before,
   Of joy, hope, love! louder and more!

VII

Nor the great flower-queen would I ask to be,
  The splendid rose, in pure blush-color dressed,
Only a drop of rain that quietly
    In her deep heart might rest.

Not the cathedral with its carven flowers,
  Its proud proportions, traceries fine and fair,
One of the humble bells that from the towers
    Gather the flock to prayer.

Not the high poet whom a Muse has kissed,
  Only some floating perfume, sound, or beam,
Some faint tint in the fading evening mist
    Might make him pause and dream.

VIII

Though true it be these splendid dreams of mine
Are but as bubbles little children blow,
And that Fate laughs to see them wax and shine,
Then holds out her pale finger — and they go:
One bitter drop falls with a tear-like gleam, —
Still, dreaming is so sweet! Still, let me dream!

Though true, to love may be definèd thus:
To open wide your safe defenceless hall
To some great guest full-armed and dangerous,
With power to ravage, to deface it all,
A cast at dice whether or no he will, —
Still, loving is so sweet! Let me love still!

IX

Thou by the river musing,
  Maid of few summer-tides,
With dreamy eyes perusing
  Thy looking-glass that glides :

Somewhere the ship is booming
  Whose hold thy treasure hides,
Somewhere the castle looming
  Where thy true love abides.

Somewhere the wreath is blowing
  To crown thy hair a bride's,
Somewhere the stout oak growing
  To make thy coffin sides.

X

THE DUST

It settles softly on your things,
　　Impalpable, fine, light, dull, grey:
Her dingy dust-clout Betty brings
　　And singing brushes it away:

And it's a queen's robe, once so proud,
　　And it's the moths fed in its fold,
It's leaves, and roses, and the shroud
　　Wherein an ancient saint was rolled.

And it is Beauty's golden hair,
　　And it is Genius' crown of bay,
And it is lips once warm and fair
　　That kissed in some forgotten May. . . .

XI

THE brain is as a treasure-chest
  Wherein the hard gold never fails,
The heart is but a mossy nest
  All full of soft young nightingales.

My gold I give thee, wear at best
  Upon thy hand, a chill bright ring,
But let my bird lie in thy breast,
  A nestling, warm, love-hungry thing.

XII

THE sun in the pine is sleeping, sleeping,
  The drops of resin gleam. . . .
There's a mighty wizard with perfumes keeping
  My brain benumbed in a dream!

The wind in the pine is rushing, rushing,
  Fine and unfettered and wild. . . .
There's a mighty mother imperiously hushing
  Her fretful, uneasy child!

XIII

I LIE and stare, I lie and stare,
  And what I feared seems fast my lot:
  I call thee, and thou comest not,
I seek thee, and thou art not there.

Art thou, Sleep, as the worldling is,
  Friends only with the lightsome heart?
  And is it writ thou shalt depart
All eyelids Care hath marked for his?

Then go.   Less sadly I resign
  Thine offices, O cool and sweet,
  That in the end we still must meet,
And thou eternally be mine.

XIV

Still ever and again it rises,
  Still ever and again!
The dream that makes one love and hate it,
  So sweet it is and vain:

How one might seek a fair new country
  Far o'er the water's blue,
And there amid an unknown people
  Begin one's life anew!

XV

THE RIVAL

This is the hardest of my fate:
  She 's better whom he doth prefer
Than I am that he worshipped late,
  As well as so much prettier,
So much more fortunate!

He 'll not repent: oh, you will see,
  She 'll never give him cause to grieve!
I dream that he comes back to me,
  Leaving her, — but he 'll never leave!
Hopelessly sweet is she.

So that if in my place she stood,
  She 'd spare to curse him, she 'd forgive!
I loathe her, but I know she would —
  And so will I, God, as I live,
Not she alone is good!

15

XVI

My little child, love thou the rose,
  For on her satin stem,
How good, see now, how fair she shows!
By loving fair, good things, one grows
  Perchance somewhat like them.

Yet, O my little child, love too
  Yon nettle where he stands,
So spiteful, ugly, harsh to view, —
Didst thou imagine, dear, the dew
  Fell only on fertile lands?

For, little child, a nettle's fate,
  Think, how it must be sad!
And how love by the hundredweight
At best, could scarcely compensate
  For being ugly and bad.

16

XVII

And then? — Then when the roses
  Were ripe, they went to seed.
And then? — Was seen a white scar
  Where once a wound did bleed.

And then? — After a little
  Hope found she might not stay.
And then? — Then as the year waned
  The swallows went away.

And then? — They laid the hero
  Among forgotten men
Low in the lone God's-acre,
  Beneath a stone — And then? . . .

XVIII

A SPACE of sky where the eyes may find
  No edge in the restful blue,
A single flower of some sweet kind,
  A memory or two,

A hope or two, a wish or so,
  A childish trust supreme
In stars that sway our fates below, —
  And a June day's length to dream.

XIX

THE flowers fall thick upon his way;
  The crowds look at his face
As one belonging to a race
  Of taller men than they.

Henceforth a servile world will trim
  Its speech to meet his mood;
Henceforth his deeds will all seem good,
  Because they come of him.

After long impotence, lo! power;
  After long strife and strain,
Dreams of this hour long crushed for vain,
  Behold! he hath his hour.

The slave that's ever at his side,
  Noting his absent eye
Fixed vaguely between earth and sky:
  " His head is light with pride."

For once, though, hath the watch-dog erred:
  Stranger to flowers and cheers,
He doth but gaze back through the years,
  And wonder, " Hath she heard? "

XX

I so love life, for the sake of life,
And breath for the love of breath,
A song for the splendid sake of song,
A word for what it saith.

For no far end, no gain, no pleasure,
Nor good that comes thereof :
But measured words just for worded measure
I love — for the sake of love.

XXI

Seas that a pale light lies on,
And clear against the pale
    Horizon,
A fleeing chalk-white sail. . . .

Across the sunburnt meadows,
The fringe of living green
    That shadows
A rill that sings unseen. . . .

The brown pond dim and stilly
Where, anchored safe and deep,
    A lily
Has shut herself to sleep. . . .

ACE OF FAIRYGOLD

XXII

LAST night when stars their softest shone,
One came to me in dream and said,
  " Forlorn thy days are, Loving One,
    For I have long been dead.

" And I who lived so long ago,
My earthly days, too, were forlorn,
  For thou whom I had cherished so
    Hadst not yet then been born."

23

XXIII

Far better than a great gift granted
    Is, to my thought,
A little gift, not asked, not wanted,
    From one that owes one naught.

Had I the giving of some great gift,
    It should be spent
On one with never a hope to lift
    To aught so magnificent.

XXIV

ROCKING-SONG

FLIGHTS of white cloud pigeons,
  Flocks of white cloud sheep,
Float o'er the hills of heaven
  And in its pastures sleep. . . .

Thirteen little linnets
  Lived in one same nest,
Nor ever asked their mother
  Which was prettiest. . . .

Scores of dark-eyed pansies
  Blossomed side by side,
The butterfly most favored
  One that was cross-eyed. . . .

25

Some say that every cricket
  Plays on a mandolin,
And that the fine moth miller
  Is not what he has been. . . .

Come, let us seek together
  The palace of the King,
There, in the treasure-chamber
  Is such a pretty thing. . . .

But all around are warders,
  And such stout watch they keep
No little child can enter —
  Except he be asleep. . . .

Then close thy pretty eyelids,
  My tender friend, and rest,
So we shall see the wonders
  In the King's treasure-chest! . . .

XXV

DEARER than rubies beading
  A Pharaonid's crown,
A rosy hope by whose light
  To rise and to lie down.

Even in its soft seceding
  From worlds of dim dream-shine,
My soul exclaims, " Good-morning,
  Beautiful hope of mine ! "

On seas of sleep receding,
  Ship almost out of sight!
My soul sends its last message,
  " Beautiful hope, good-night ! "

XXVI

WHEN I was little I used to gaze
  Where in the deep, dark air
The white stars used to blink and blaze
Like friendly, sleepy diamond eyes,
  And wonder what they were.

And now it has been all explained,
  The mystery of a star, —
And still with eyelids upward strained
I stand with my dull knowledge gained
  And wonder what they are.

XXVII

Then lead me, Friend.   Here is my hand,
  Not in dumb resignation lent
Because Thee one cannot withstand —
  In love, Lord, with complete consent.

Lead, and I, not as one born blind
  Obeys in sheer necessity,
But one with muffled eyes designed,
  Will blindly trust myself to Thee.

Lead.   Though the road Thou mak'st me tread
  Bring sweat of anguish to my brow,
And on the flints my track be red,
  I will not murmur.   It is Thou.

Lead.   If we come to the cliff's crest,
  And I hear deep below — O deep ! —
The torrent's roar, and " Leap ! " Thou say'st,
  I will not question — I will leap.

XXVIII

We talked of life and death. She said,
"Whichever of us two first dies
Shall come back from among the dead
And teach his friend these mysteries."

She died last night. And all this day
I swear that things of every kind
Are trying, trying to convey
Some message to my troubled mind.

I looked up from my tears erewhile :
That white rose dying in the cup
Was gazing at me with her smile, —
It blushed her blush as I looked up.

It paled then with an agony
Of effort to express me aught
That would, I think, bring peace to me,
Could I but grasp — But I cannot.

And when the wind rose, at my door
  It clamored with a plaintive din,
Like some poor creature begging sore
  To be let in — I let it in.

It blew the light out; round my head
  It whirled, and swiftly in my ear
Had whispered something ere it fled —
  It had her voice, so low, so dear.

The looking-glass this livelong day
  Has worn that curious meaning air;
I feel it when I look away
  Reflecting things that are not there.

Now long no breath of wind has stirred,
  Yet bends the lamp-flame as if fanned;
The clock says o'er and o'er a word —
  But I, God! — cannot understand!

XXIX

TRULY, sometimes my heart, even mine, is lead,
But no one ever knows that I am sad.

I dare not tell my woe to those I love
Lest they be shadowed by the gloom thereof,

And those that love not me, how should I dare
To burden them with my despisèd care?

XXX

Be good to me ! If all the world united
    Should bend its powers to gird my youth with
      pain,
Still might I fly to thee, Dear, and be righted —
    But if thou wrong'st me, where shall I complain?

I am the dove a random shot surprises,
    That from her flight she droppeth quivering,
And in the deadly arrow recognizes
    A blood-wet feather — once in her own wing.

XXXI

A LILY grew beside a pool
  Whose depths were dark and foul enow,
And cast on it the beautiful
  Reflection of her stainless brow :

Then loved it, for it seemed to her
  A thing so full of worth and grace
That turned up to the traveller
  That innocent and tender face.

XXXII

At the cross-roads, in green April,
　　Paused the hero doubtfully :
Up one sunlit road stood Glory
　　Smiling 'neath a laurel-tree.

And the knight cried, "Thou art lovely,
　　Thou art all a queen," cried he,
"And thou smilest, and I worship,
　　But I will not go to thee.

" Down yon path where naught allureth
　　Bids the call of Chivalry, —
If at last we are together,
　　'T will be thou hast followed me."

35

XXXIII

MIDNIGHT

How I should weep were I to pause and think
Upon my little life, so gone to waste!
Fresh, sparkling draught, spilled, that the hot
sands drink. . . .
The winds shall dry it, all will be effaced! . . .
How I should weep, were I to pause and think !

I pause . . . I think . . . and tears of anguish
rise
Tumultuous from my long subduèd breast. . . .
The barren sands receive them from my eyes,
And drink them, wasted, wasted like the
rest! . . .
I pause, I think, and burning tears arise. . . .

XXXIV

THE wind had been foretelling
  Mysteriously that morn
How, soon, from Earth, the Mother,
  The sweet Spring should be born;
And sitting by the river
  From icy fetters freed,
This is what a faun piped
  Upon his hollow reed.

He piped: Soft beds of grasses
  Spread out 'neath a blue roof,
And tepid waters, soothing
  To a tired brown faun's hoof;
Broad stretches of warm sunshine,
  With lapses of cool shade,
And ripening berries making
  Red blots in a green glade.

37

He piped: One glossy cherry
  For each white blossom-star;
Long trains of dappled swallows
  Home-flying from afar;
And all the brown fauns tuning
  Their pipes for concerts sweet,
And all the meadows dimpled
  With dancing of nymphs' feet.

And then: Wild flowers springing
  Where'er a good seed blows,
And in the sheltered gardens
  That marvel, the red rose;
And singing birdlings building
  Their nests with busy pains,
And rosy little children
  Fashioning daisy-chains.

Moreover: Jewels scattered
  Lavishly on the grass;
White dew-drops in the lilacs,
  That tremble, shine, and pass;

Winds full of sweet confusion
   With hum and buzz and trill,
And lazy white clouds lolling
   Leisurely on the hill.

The old brown faun sat piping,
   The air was cold and keen,
And still he piped: A little,
   And all the trees are green!
A little! and the roses
   Break from the thorny spray!
For I heard the zephyr saying
   Spring should be born to-day.

XXXV

"'Thou smell'st not ill, thou object plain,
Thou art a small, pretentious grain
    Of amber, I suppose."
" Nay, my good friend, I am by birth
A common clod of scentless earth . . .
    But I lived with the Rose."
               (*Eastern Apologue.*)

XXXVI

Could I not be the pilgrim
To reach my saint's abode,
I would make myself the road
To lead some other pilgrim
Where my soul's treasure glowed.

Could not I in the eager van
Be the stalwart pioneer
Who points where the way is clear,
I would be the man who sinks in the swamp,
And cries to the rest, " Not here!"

XXXVII

WHAT will Time give for youth we lose,
For dense bright hair, and lip of rose,
For flowers wherewith Spring heaps our laps,
For trust in words, and faith in shows,
And all the castle-dreams he saps?

For wealth of hair, and lip of rose,
For faith in promises and shows,
For buds of May heaped in your laps,
What Time will give you? — Ah, who knows?
. . . Patience, perhaps.

XXXVIII

Love me or love me not, yet what shall hinder
My soul from breathing blessings on thy name?
    Be far less kind, or oh, so little kinder,
        My love will be the same.

Nor need she care, the Empress great and
        golden,
When she with sleep her beauty doth restore,
    And dreams, in jealous majesty enfolden,
        What slave lies at her door.

XXXIX

Is it that as Youth's dreams retreat
  And quench in gloom their phantom glitter,
As life becomes not all so sweet
  Death seems not either quite so bitter? . . .

XL

WHEN comes the fearful hour that I must die,
　Remember, Lord, how merciful I was, —
I never meant to hurt a thing, — not I,
　The creatures that I spared will plead my cause.

Then slay me softly, make me not to be
　As I have sometimes seen a drop of light
Fall from among the still stars silently,
　And cease upon the breathless summer night.

XLI

To be a little child once more
  And in its dreamless cradle lie,
To hear a soft voice o'er and o'er
  Refraining, "Bye-low-baby-bye,"

To be a child! be innocence
  Of all that hath man's heart beguiled,
Yet know by some mysterious sense
  How good it is to be a child!

XLII

When Spring has come, and in your frost-bound
  heart
Is born with her first sighing o'er the hills
The longing that so strangely softens it,
The blind, warm reaching out toward all that lives
And breathes the tepid air along with you,
The dreamy joy in life and youth and things
That swells your aching breast and finds no
  words, —
Thrice happy, oh, thrice happy still the Earth
That can express herself in roses, yea,
Can make the lily tell her inmost thought!

XLIII

O FANCIES mine, O butterflies,
You seem so fine when high in air,
I guess you sweet, I dream you fair,
    With foolish following eyes.

The world, then, must inspect your dyes :
And so the chase is swift and hot;
I laugh at length when you are caught,
    Poor flimsy butterflies.

Alas! the net has torn your wings! . . .
My hand, you are so frail and faint,
Has brushed off half your pretty paint,
    Small, soft, misusèd things.

Arranged with pitiful ado
In a pretentious little book,
How different, how tame you look! —
    And yet I love you, too.

XLIV

IN THE ART MUSEUM

HE stands where the white light showers,
  In his wonted high recess ;
The dust has woven a soft veil
  Over his comeliness.

Beneath the pensive eyebrows
  And lids that never beat,
The same glance floats forever,
  So sad and solemn-sweet ;

The same peace seals forever
  The full lips finely curled —
I 'm come to this his dwelling
  To bring him news of the world:

" Once more the Spring hath mantled
  With green the lasting hills —
Hast thou no faint remembrance
  Of daisies and daffodils?

"Their stems still lengthen sunward
  As when thou wast of us —
My heart swells with its sorrow
  For thee, Antinous."

XLV

THE Sun looked from his everlasting skies,
He laughed into my daily-dying eyes :
He said to me, the brutal shining sun,
" Poor, fretful, hot, rebellious, little one !

" Thou shalt not find it, yet there shall be truth.
Thou shalt grow old, but yet there shall be
     youth,
Thou shalt not do, yet great deeds shall be
     done, —
Believe me, child, I am an old, old Sun !

" Thou mayst go blind, yet fair will bloom the
     Spring,
Thou mayst not hear them, but the birds will
     sing,
Thou mayst despair, no less will hope be rife,
Thou must lie dead, but many will have life.

51

" Thou mayst declare of love : it is a dream!
Yet long with love, my love, the Earth, will
    teem —
Let not thy foolish heart be borne so low,
Lift up thy heart!   Exult that it is so ! "

XLVI

EASTERN AIRS

I

LIFE 's but a day, then let 's be joyous
   And wisely spend our shining day ;
There is a boatman shall convoy us
   At eve to shores where all is grey —
We 'll grieve less that he leaves no toy us
   If we are tired out with play !

XLVII

II

I KNOW a garden full of roses,
    Oh, roses of the deepest dye!
That on three sides a wall encloses,
    The fourth a river washes by.
There, face of beauty, Morning Eye!
    To rest at noontide fain were I,
Having thy voice between our dozes
    To soothe me with an ancient lie. . . .

XLVIII

III

RATHER, O Falcon Eyes, the gleaner said,
The cloud for curtain to my bed,
And only what is gleaned for bread,
And bare feet and bare head,
Than be a daughter of the great,
And on a bed inlaid with pearl
Eat rose-paste from a silver plate —
And thou the lover of another girl!

XLIX

AT A WINDOW

Our earth with its proud mountains draped
In snow we call eternal, and the time thereof,
   Are unto God as in the sea one tear —
      The things that shall not be escaped
         Is not it, pensive love,
      As if already they were here?

Already each in his sealed hermitage
We lie, that yet were social! grass above;
   The story of our lives, so full of things!
      Abridged to fit one marble page;
And yearly twice a kindly person brings
Brave wreaths for us, in pious pilgrimage. . . .

Already what was flesh of ours has climbed to
    light
    In daisies that with round gold eyes
Stare at our house's sign, no longer white :
They could not read it, were they human-wise,
    So are the letters filled with moss,
So have the summer creatures woven webs
    across. . . .

Already we are trampled to the plain,
A silent, wind-swept desert; then,
The air is shivered with the shouts of men,
Ploughs scatter us, wheels grind us further down,
    Above us grows the town. . . .

    Dear Heart, these gauds of life, are they so
      dear
    To us, dear Heart, to us . . . already dead?
      The curious jewel for the ear,
      The flashing fillet for the head?
And, treasures that all in their kind excel,
This fair well-painted fan, this scarf so well
    embroidered? . . .

57

Nay, Love, but the great house itself, builded so
    well,
    That speaks in every part a master's touch,
        Is it so much? . . .
    Nay, Love, but everything and everything,
    However precious, that must surely die
And with the eyes that looked on it lie mould-
    ering,
Is it so great it cannot mutely be laid by? . . .

    Behold! less will I love them, toys of death,
    But you I will love more, love on and on! —
For "Heaven and Earth shall pass," saith One,
      "But not my Word," He saith.
It is His word that this in you and me
With which we love shall live eternally. . . .

L

When after the long dark story
　　Of desperate wars to wage
The King shall have come to his heritage
　　Of power and pleasure and glory,

He'll travel back, gold-shodden,
　　The steep track to the throne,
That with bare feet and many a groan
　　Of old by him was trodden.

He'll say to each least sweet flower
　　That lined the rugged way,
" Thou cheered'st me in my darksome day,
　　Be blessed this golden hour! "

He'll pause by the homely briar
　　That shielded him in storm :
" Be blessed, O humble, friendly form
　　That shivered the tempest's ire! "

His face in its kingly glory
    Shall bend o'er the poor stream's brink :
" Be blessed, O stream that gav'st me drink
    When I was a pilgrim sorry!"

And then to the sharp stones even
    That made the road so hard,
He 'll say, " Sharp stones o'er which I far'd,
    Be blessed !   I have forgiven."

LI

O STRIKE the lyre in minor key,
  And let sad songs ascend,
For each man's life is a tragedy —
  The hero dies in the end.

The nightingale sings in the tree . . .
  Disciple, crouch beneath:
The nightingale what singeth she
  But songs of love and death?

LII

THE LASTING ROSE

I

WHEN ways are foul with trodden snow,
  And flaying winds drive through the street,
And blue-lipped, muffled people go
  With cautious, cramped, uncertain feet,

You see behind a misted pane
  Great clouds of green and pink and red,
You enter, and find Spring again,
  Soft air, spoils of a garden-bed :

When other ways, with other snows
  Are bad to walk, and harshly free
Through life's sad locks the bleak wind
    blows . . .
  Turn to the books of poetry.

62

LIII

II

FLORIST that never closes!
  Flowers that never fall!
But fair unfailing roses
  And lilies sculptural;

Geraniums fixed in flaming,
  Consummate violets
Confirmed in bloom, disclaiming
  Laws of a sun that sets!

Undone the clasps! We greet thee,
  Realm of the lasting rose,
Blessed poetry! and cheat thee,
  Cold circumstance, grey prose!

63

LIV

SEE in the sun-steeped garden-bed
  How gay the summer rose!
And on what long-hushed lip it's fed
  Nobody knows.

One laughs with all her pretty teeth,
  So happy! they suppose,
And of the heart-break underneath
  Nobody knows.

Lightly one reads a little song,
  And all the dreaming goes
To make a ditty twelve lines long
  Nobody knows.

LV

MAID, when thou walk'st in Spring-time,
  Cast down thy simple eyes,
By no means let them follow
  Two wandering butterflies;

Ignore all tender nonsense
  The warm wind may suggest,
Avoid to watch the swallows
  Building their little nest;

The sweet seductive roses
  Consider at no price:
A glowing rose might give thee
  Some ill-advised advice!

LVI

TO A WEED

You bold thing! thrusting 'neath the very nose
Of her fastidious majesty, the rose,
Even in the best ordainèd garden bed,
Unauthorized, your smiling little head!

The gardener, mind! will come in his big boots,
And drag you up by your rebellious roots,
And cast you forth to shrivel in the sun,
Your daring quelled, your little weed's life done.

And when the noon cools, and the sun drops
     low,
He 'll come again with his big wheelbarrow,
And trundle you — I don't know clearly where,
But off, outside the dew, the light, the air.

Meantime — ah, yes! the air is very blue,
And gold the light, and diamond the dew, —
You laugh and courtesy in your worthless way,
And you are gay, ah, so exceeding gay!

You argue in your manner of a weed,
You did not make yourself grow from a seed,
You fancy you've a claim to standing-room,
You dream yourself a right to breathe and
   bloom.

The sun loves you, you think, just as the rose,
He never scorned you for a weed, — he knows!
The green-gold flies rest on you and are glad,
It's only cross old gardeners find you bad.

You know, you weed, I quite agree with you,
I am a weed myself, and I laugh too, —
Both, just as long as we can shun his eye,
Let's sniff at the old gardener trudging by!

67

LVII

Ah, worshipped one, ah, faithful Spring!
Again you come, again you bring
That flock of flowers from the fold
Where warm it slept, while we were cold.

What shall we say to one so dear,
Who keeps her promise every year?
Ah, hear me promise! and as true
As you to us, am I to you:

Ne'er shall you come and as a child
Sit in the market piping mild,
With dance suggestion in your glance
And I not dance — and I not dance!

But you the same will always be,
While ninety Springs will alter me;
Yet surely as you come and play,
So surely will I dance, I say!

68

There is a strange thing to be seen
One distant April pink and green :
Before a young child piping sweet,
An old child dancing with spent feet. . . .

LVIII

THY heart the dove-cote is, and mine the dove,
  That still on faithful wing returns at eve,
And in thy heart, still open to receive,
    Finds rest and long, long tranquil dreams of
      love. . . .

Thou fearful image! cease now from my brain!
  What wilt then thou with me? Show me no
    more
That storm-blown dove that beats her breast in
    vain
    And bleeds against a blind unanswering
      door! . . .

For his heart is the dove-cote, mine the dove,
  That still on steadfast wings shall come at eve,
And in his heart, still wide, wide to receive,
    Shall rest and dream long dreams of happy
      love.

LIX

You may be blue and blue and blue,
   Up there! blue as you please,
And boast a sun that smelting low
   Refines you into gold,
And song-birds may send up to you
   A million melodies! . . .
But I know, I know what I know,
   I am not to be consoled.

LX

One wanted so much to be glorious!
    An organ great and sweet;
He could be but humbly cheerful,
    An organ of the street!
It trundled on, hammering bravely
    Airs not at all sublime:
Where'er it chanced, the children danced,
    The grown folk stepped in time.

LXI

WELL to remember, standing in the light
   Of fortune's smile, so sweet one dreams it
      true!
Them that in shadow with the vultures fight,
   Devouring at their hopes, forever new.

Good to remember, groping in the night
   To find the passage leading from despair,
Them that afar walk on a sunlit height
   Rejoicing in the prospect, the pure air. . . .

LXII

Sleep, O Marie!   Lean that pale, drooping head
  Against this pillow I have smoothed for thee,
While I will sit and watch beside thy bed,
    Poor, poor Marie!

The lamp made such a hard glare where it stood,
  I 've shaded it and placed it not so near.
Now thou hast closed thine eyes, now it is good,
    Shall I sing, dear?

        Once, dear, it came to me,
          Once in the night,
      ˙ That in his Paradise
        Christ had thought, Christ-wise,
        To make a paradise —
        So, dear, it came to me,
          Once in the night, —

Another paradise,
  Not quite so bright,
But stiller, shadier,
Just for those wearier
Poor souls that must prefer
To His bright Paradise
  One not so bright!

LXIII

STORY-BOOK

I

SINCE Sir Gilfred, unforgiven,
   Spurred his mad steed from her gate,
Day by day the Lady's song grows
    Louder, lighter;

And even as its mirth increases,
   In the burnished oval plate
Day by day the Lady's cheek shows
    Thinner, whiter.

LXIV

II

Poor Fra Gentile, when the almonds bloom,
Stands shuddering in the Spring light, golden
warm,
Both hands cramped on his heart to still the
storm
Roused in it by that stealing May perfume. . . .

Then with wide helpless eyes that cannot see,
For hours and hours he walks the cloister brown,
Battling to crush it out, to tread it down,
That old tormenting, tender memory.

LXV

III

Speaks the wizard to his minion,
  Nightly, " Fly now without rest,
Penetrate the distant castle,
  Spy upon the Loveliest ! "

Through the narrow crystal channel
  Hardly once the sands have run,
When before his chafing master
  Bows the imp, his errand done.

" Spite of sentinel and watch-dog,
  To the Fair One's bower I crept;
In a moonbeam she lay sleeping, —
  She had prayed before she slept."

" Teasing fiend ! Accursèd spirit !
  Bringest ever evil news,
Whilst the maiden is so minded
  Magic spells I vainly use ! "

78

LXVI

IV

How dreary looks the ivied cot,
  (Yet all is flush with May!)
How sad the little garden plot,
  Since Mary went away.

At morning to her window-side
  A flock of sparrows comes:
They wait and wonder, "Where can bide
  That Mary of the crumbs?"

Below, the poor neglected flowers
  In languid whispers sigh,
" Where is that Mary of the showers,
  Will she come bye and bye?"

And every night down in the lane,
  Just past the gate, there stands
A youth whose face, wet with his pain,
  Is hidden in his hands.

www.ingramcontent.com/pod-product-compliance
Lightning Source LLC
Chambersburg PA
CBHW020257090426
42735CB00009B/1115